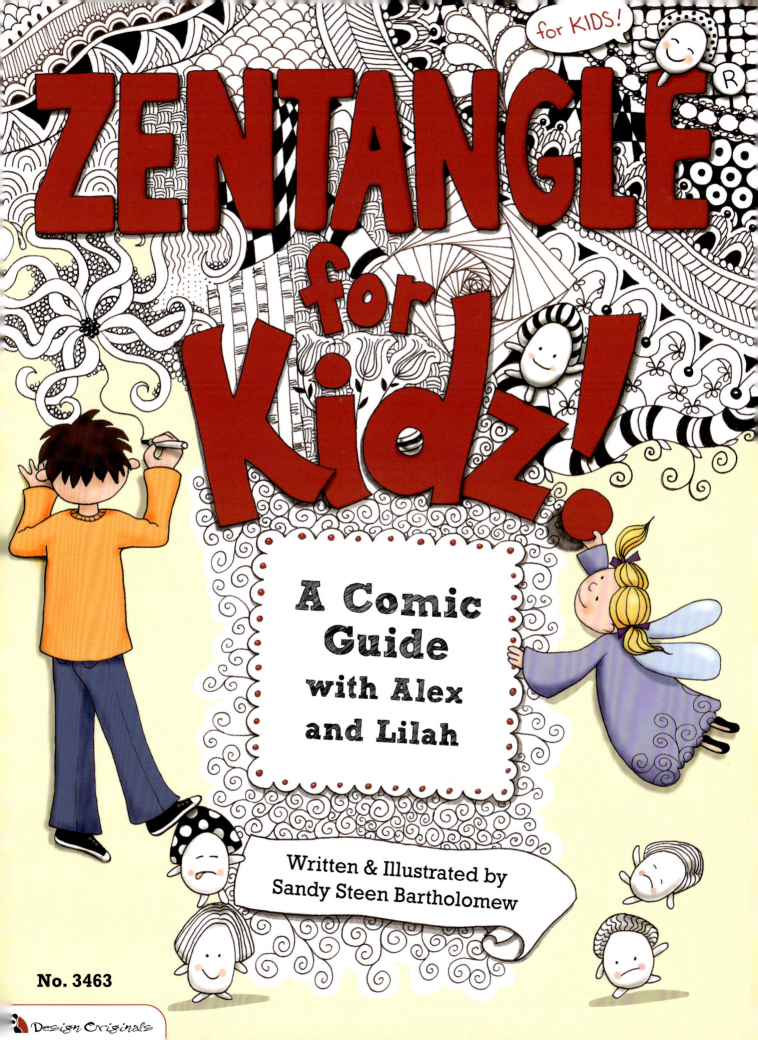

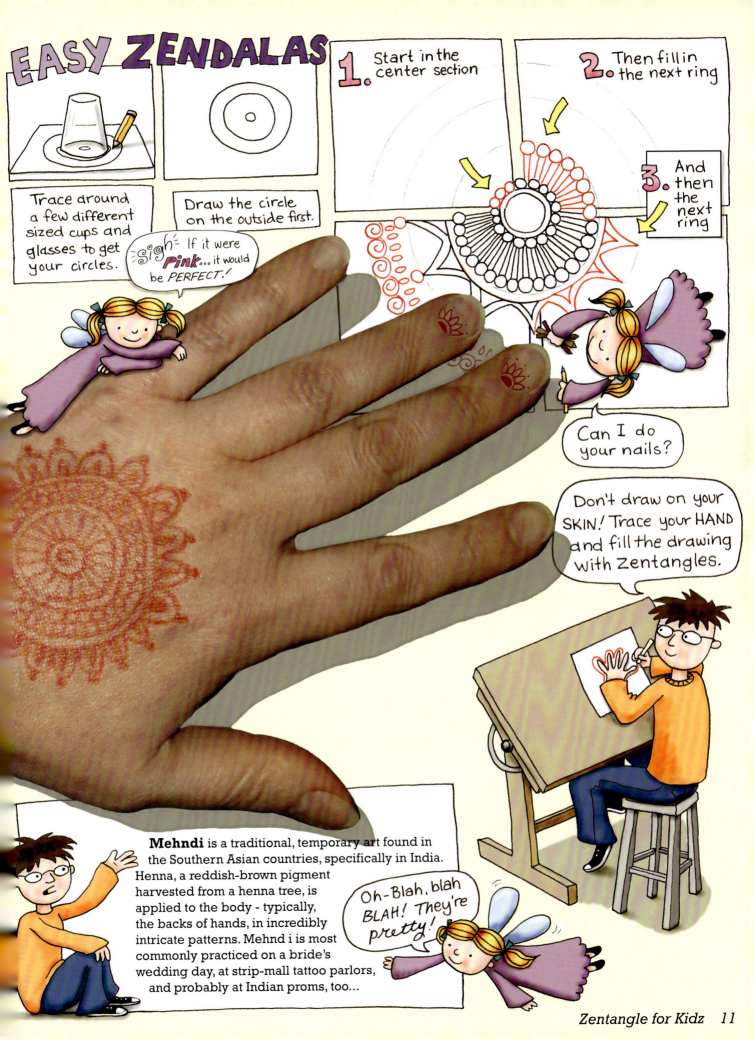

How do I keep track of all these TANGLES?

"and still have time to take over the world?!"

"and make everything pink and fluffy?"

"Meow?"

punch out hole

Photocopy this page onto cardstock and use these designs as templates.

Tangle

Steps

Design By

Use a metal ring, or a paper clip, to hold a whole bunch of tags together.

These Tangle Trading Cards will fit in plastic baseball card collector pages.

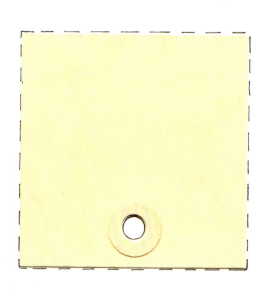

18   Zentangle for Kidz

ART/Techniques/Drawing $8.99 US

Praise for this book:

Anyone can learn Zentangle®. Even an adult. But this is the best book ever written for kids. Maybe *not* for little sisters... they shouldn't have this much power. —Alex, age 13

It would be *much* better if the cover was pink! —Lilah, age 4

Other books by Sandy Steen Bartholomew

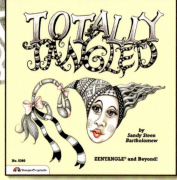

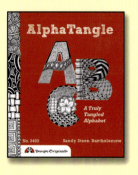

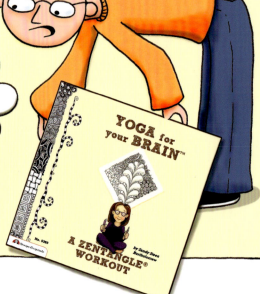

No. 3463

Design Originals
an Imprint of Fox Chapel Publishing
www.d-originals.com

ISBN: 978-1-57421-340-9